POGO

by

Walt Kelly

POGO

VOLUME **1**

by

Walt Kelly

FANTAGRAPHICS BOOKS

FANTAGRAPHICS BOOKS

7563 Lake City Way NE
Seattle WA 98115

Edited by Gary Groth
Design and Production by Pat Moriarity
Cover color separations by Port Publications
Thanks to Steve Thompson and Rick Norwood for historical and archival assistance
Published by Gary Groth and Kim Thompson

First Fantagraphics Books edition: July 1992
Second Fantagraphics Books edition: April 1999

ISBN: 1-56097-018-9

Printed in the U.S.A.

INTRODUCING *Walt Kelly* by R.C. HARVEY

For those of you who are prowling this page knowing that Walt Kelly was one of the few authentic geniuses to work in the comic strip medium, Kelly needs no introduction. You may skip to the good stuff. And if you came in here seeking to ascertain the accuracy of the rumor you've heard about his genius, the best testimony begins a few pages to the right — the good stuff. Kelly's *Pogo*.

Still, for you newcomers — and for the sake of *auld lang syne* — let us take a couple of minutes to reprise a refrain or two of praise in appreciation of Kelly by way of setting the mood for the good stuff that follows.

Let us say it as unequivocally as possible: Walt Kelly earned himself a place in the pantheon of the medium's greatest practitioners by demonstrating indisputably that, in the right hands, comics can be high art. And for a quarter of a century, Kelly's hands were the right ones.

It's scarcely enough to describe *Pogo* as a ''funny animal strip'' set in a southern swamp. In Kelly's hands, the strip transcended the funny animal strip tradition (as perpetuated in such strips as *Bugs Bunny* and *Donald Duck* — even *Animal Crackers*). At its core, Kelly's strip was a reincarnation of vaudeville, and its routines were often laced with humor that derived from pure slapstick. To that, Kelly added the remarkably fanciful and inventive language of his characters — a ''southern fried'' dialect that lent itself readily to his characters' propensity to take things literally and permitted an unblinking delight in puns.

An animal strip, yes, but Kelly's animals were more than animals. They were perfectly content being

animals, you understand, but sometimes on an otherwise idle summer's afternoon, they would (for their own amusement) try out for roles as human beings. They'd wander backstage at the human drama, picking up a script here, a bit of costume there, and then assemble after hours before the footlights for a little play-acting. But somehow it never quite came off as intended.

We, the human spectators, could recognize some of the parts being assayed, but there was always something vaguely out of kilter. The animal actors had picked up the jargon and the costumes, but they didn't seem to understand the purpose in any of the human endeavors they mimicked.

So they would make up reasons, rationales, as they went along — discarding perfectly sound, human, reasons for everything they did in favor of some of their own invention.

Sometimes, to derive purposes that made sense to them, they attached meaning and significance to words, taken literally, rather than to the ideas the words represented. Adrift in misunderstood figures of speech, mistaken identities, and double entendres going off in all directions at once, Kelly's creatures wandered further and further from what appeared to have been their original intentions.

One thing led to another by free association leapfrog: it made a wonderful kind of logic all its own, but it left motivation in tatters somewhere along the wayside. An episode in the fall of 1950 began with the swamp's wholesale courtship of a skunk that turned into a brief panic about sea serpents that became a migration West that subjected everyone momentarily to the ministrations of the resident con man that resulted, finally, in a cow taking work as a cat.

But you had to be there: it loses a lot in the telling.

Easily distracted (from even the scripts they'd apparently undertaken to enact), the residents of Kelly's swamp needed almost no encouragement to abandon the human roles they'd taken up so lightly in order to bask in the friendly glow of a fish-fry and perloo. In the fellowship of the feasting, the animals regained their good and common sense: concentrating upon the meat-and-potatoes of existence presumably regenerated them after the strain of behaving nonsensically like humans.

And that was the trick of Kelly's social satire: we couldn't help but glimpse ourselves in his menagerie — looking just as silly as we often are. But if the animals knew we were silly, they didn't often let on. They, after all, didn't take life as seriously as we: ''It ain't nohow permanent," as Kelly — or was it Porkypine? — used to say.

All of this is funny enough in itself, but Kelly went even further in honing the satirical cutting edge of his humor. As time wended onward, Kelly added political commentary to his social satire. In the early 1950s, the double meaning of the puns in the strip took on political as well as social implications, and the vaudeville routines frequently looked suspiciously like animals imitating people high in government.

Just so we wouldn't miss the point, Kelly underscored his satirical intent with caricature: his animals had plastic features that seemed to change before our very eyes until they resembled those at whom the satire was directed. And the species suggested something about Kelly's opinions of his targets. Soviet boss Khrushchev showed up one time as a pig; Cuba's Castro, as a goat. And Richard Nixon's acid-tongued vice president, Spiro Agnew, appeared as a uniformed hyena; the implacable J. Edgar Hoover, as a bulldog.

One consequence of this technique was that the verbal and the visual, the words and the pictures, were perfectly, inseparably, wedded — the very emblem of excellence in the art of the comic strip.

We'll see it all unfold here — in this and subsequent volumes of the Fantagraphics series that will reprint the entire run of Kelly's legacy, that long and lyric masterwork in which the artform of the comic stip was raised to its ultimate. But Kelly did not reach these heights all at once at the very beginning of *Pogo*. It took him awhile. He grew up to it, then blossomed into full flower in the midst of the long summer afternoon of the Eisenhower fifties. Still, the seeds for that flowering had been sown long before even the strips in this volume were first published. They were sown in Kelly's youthful enterprises in the newspapering game while in high school, in his apprenticeship at the Walt Disney Studios, and in his journeyman labors for the burgeoning comic book industry.

Kelly was an amusing and lucid writer of prose as well as a master cartoonist, and over the years he committed several autobiographical essays, most of which masqueraded as biography written by some anonymous author. Here's a typical tongue-in-cheek production: "The first two years of Walt Kelly's life were spent in idleness. This statement is not to be confused with the statement: The first two years of Walt Kelly's life were spent in Philadelphia. Both are true but the first is regrettable and the second is not. If a man must squander his youth, it can be done in Philadelphia with dignity and thrift."

Born August 25, 1913, Walter Crawford Kelly, Jr., squandered only his infancy in the City of Brotherly Love and then moved with his parents to Bridgeport, Connecticut, where his father had obtained work in the Remington Arms munition plant.

Eschewing idleness in this fresh venue, young Walt improved his natural drawing ability by constant practice until, at the age of thirteen, he sold his first political cartoon to the *Bridgeport Post*. By the time he was attending Warren Harding High School, he held an afterschool job at the paper as a campus stringer, reporting school news and sports. At school, he was an associate editor of the school newspaper, and he did a great deal of artwork for it and for the yearbook — "under the impression that he was taking Algebra One," as Kelly put it later in an autobiographical essay.

He graduated high school in 1930 and found work wrapping scrap cloth and sweeping up in a ladies' underwear factory. After three years of this scanty employment, he secured a job as a reporter at the *Post*. Kelly was always proud of his experience as a newspaperman; in fact, Selby Kelly, his widow, said he was prouder of having been a reporter than he was of his talent and success as a world-famous cartoonist. Throughout his life, Kelly's closest friends were journalists. He sought and enjoyed the fellowship of newspapermen and spent most of his recreational hours in their company.

Kelly had not been on the job long before he was drafted into doing some artwork in addition to his reportorial assignments. The task was to illustrate the life of the legendary promoter and circus mogul, P.T. Barnum, the city's most celebrated home-town boy. This biographical effusion took the form of a comic strip with the illustration running as separate panels above a text narrative. It was an assignment that threatened to be prolonged into a life's work, Kelly said: "Every time the writer got P.T. Barnum to the death bed, old P.T. would get a flash and his entire life would [start to] pass again before his eyes" for another six-month run of the strip.

After a year or so of this, Kelly left the paper and worked for a short time as a clerk and inspector for the Department of Public Welfare, then as a clerk in an art store. Then he left Bridgeport to try freelancing his art in New York City, where, he said, he "starved quietly."

This history of his peripatetic vocational pursuits betrays all the signs of a man desperate to improve his lot. And that, doubtless, was the case with Kelly. He had fallen in love with Helen DeLacy, who worked for the Girl Scout Council in Bridgeport, and in leaving the newspaper for less glamorus sounding employment, Kelly was clearly seeking the kind of "steady work" and regular pay that would qualify him to ask for her hand in marriage. The trip to the Big Apple was the action of a young man driven by the relative inadequacy of his luck in Bridgeport to gamble on his talent in an allout try for success and fame — or, at least, financial security — in America's mecca for artists. Before that could pay off, though, Helen was transferred from Bridgeport to Los Angeles. In late 1935, Kelly packed up his meager belongings and followed his heart westward.

If you were a cartoonist on the West Coast in the Great Depression of the 1930s, chances are you worked in the Mouse Factory. On January 6, 1936, Kelly joined the growing staff at the Walt Disney Studios. ("The WPA of the cartooning world," he called it later.) His first assignment was in the story department, developing storylines, comic sequences, and assorted funny "business'' for animated cartoons. It was regular work with a decent paycheck ($100 a week — munificent for Depression times), so Kelly's courtship of Helen went forward apace — that is, with whatever haste the seemly decorum of the times would permit. And so, a year and a half later in September 1937, they married.

In the latter part of 1939, Kelly asked to be transferred to animation; his contention was that he'd be a better storyman if he knew more about animation. Disney approved, and Kelly became an animator, assisting Fred Moore. What Kelly learned as an animator that would shape his talent as a cartoonist is open, somewhat, to speculation. His later funny animal work carries none of the earmarks of the Disney style. But he couldn't help but learn something: the Disney training program was rigorous and exacting and thorough. We'll explore its operation and possible effects on Kelly's work in the next volume of this series.

Kelly was something of an odd duck around the Disney lot. Most of his colleagues followed the informal fashion of Southern California in their attire, but Kelly always dressed for business — dark suit, bow tie. With his little moustache and glasses, he looked (his friends said) like the political cartoonists' symbolic John Q. Public. But Kelly made numerous friends among his fellow workers (including, especially, Moore and Ward Kimball, who was destined to become one of the legendary ''Nine Old Men'' of Disney animation). And he joined enthusiastically in the outbreaks of horseplay that infected the place in those days whenever the cartoonists sought relief from the tedium of producing thousands of drawings, each one only slightly different from the last.

They played touch football games during the noon hour and staged practical jokes at inopportune moments. Kelly and Kimball played tin whistles and took every opportunity to rehearse. And they all circulated gag cartoons in which caricatures of themselves cavorted in wild abandon — sometimes staging monstrous touch football games, sometimes orchestras of tin

whistles. Silly stuff. And sometimes a little pornographic. Except for Kelly's. Kelly's were never pornographic. ''You couldn't tell Walt a dirty joke,'' Kimball said years later. ''He was pretty naive about backroom humor.'' The surviving Kelly sketches depict Kelly and Kimball and Moore performing a variety of roles as musicians or actors in theatrical productions.

As much as Kelly enjoyed the fellowship he found at Disney, he was not entirely happy there, according to Kimball. Animated cartooning is assembly-line work: the final product is the result of hundreds of contributions by others. Cartoonists who work in animation suppress their personalities and styles in order to produce the standard product. And this was not the sort of work Kelly was suited for. He was looking for some way to escape when the notorious labor dispute erupted in the spring of 1941.

The Disney operation had grown too large for its founder to be personally involved in every aspect of its daily life. The less his employees saw of him, the more they could find fault with their working conditions. To seek redress, they wanted to form a union. Disney said he had no objection but wanted them to conduct union business — voting and the like — off the premises. Privately, he was outraged. He had a paternalistic attitude toward his employees — the remnant of the days when he and his workers were in daily contact, engaged in the momentous undertaking of renovating and defining animated cartooning — and he couldn't believe they would turn against him after all they'd been through together. The strike was bitter and prolonged: the first picket line was set up May 29, and the strike lasted through the summer into September. The Disney Studio was never the same thereafter. The atmosphere of affectionate collegiality and mutual enterprise — the sense of making a common cause together — that had once pervaded the place evaporated in the heat of disputation and its wake.

For Kelly, that first picket line was the last straw. He had friends on both sides of the line and didn't want

to support either at the expense of the other. Claiming family problems (his sister was ill), he took a leave of absence and was back East in a few days. Helen followed him as soon as she could. Kelly never returned. Offically, he went off the Disney payroll on September 12.

He and Helen set up housekeeping in Nichols, Connecticut, near Bridgeport. They moved often during the first few months, settling eventually in Darien. Kelly commuted to New York to find freelance work. In his occasional letters to Kimball, Kelly sounded grim about his prospects. He was struggling to pry loose a living at his trade. Exactly what he was doing we don't know. Not much identifiable Kelly artwork has surfaced from this period. Helen said that Walt Disney helped him find work at Western Printing and Lithographing Company where Disney and Dell comic books were printed. But the first comic book work that's clearly Kelly's didn't get into print until late 1942. It is likely that he tried to make his own way without using a referral from Disney for a period, perhaps 10-12 months. In any event, identifiable Kelly art appeared in the first issue of *Animal Comics*, copyrighted in 1942 and appearing on the newsstands at the end of that year. For scholars of cartooning, it was a historic moment: on its pages, Kelly limned Pogo Possum for the first time. (About which, more in a subsequent volume of this series.)

Kelly worked in comic books for most of the decade, creating material for several Dell titles. In addition to *Animal Comics*, he drew for *Our Gang, The Brownies, Raggedy Ann and Andy, Santa Claus Funnies*, and *Easter with Mother Goose*. And he drew covers for *Walt Disney's Comics & Stories* as well as occasional interior stories. Apart from his work in comic books, he illustrated some children's books for Julian Messner, Inc., using the pseudonym Tony Maclay. During World War II, Kelly's health prevented active military service (he'd had rheumatic fever as a child), but as a civilian, he illustrated dictionaries and language guidebooks for the Foreign Language Unit, Army Language Section, U.S.

Army Education Branch of the Army Service Forces.

Upon his return to the Bridgeport environs, Kelly renewed his friendship with an old *Post* chum, Niles White von Wettberg, who introduced him to John Horn. Horn, like Von Wettberg, was working as a sports researcher for *Newsweek*. Childhood illnesses had rendered all three men ineligible for military service, and they had much else in common. They shared a passion for newspapering, and they loved to talk politics in bars. For the next twenty years, the three of them had lunch together at least once a week in one or another of Manhattan's most convivial saloons.

After the War, John Horn was working at *Argosy* as cartoon and photo editor. During several of their lunches, he urged Kelly to try his hand at gag cartoons. Kelly did so, but he said he really preferred political cartooning to magazine gag cartooning. He did a batch of political cartoons and showed them to Horn and Von Wettberg. Horn took them to a former boss, George Y. Wells, *Newsweek*'s press editor, suggesting that Wells propose Kelly as a new political cartoonist for the *New York Herald Tribune*, where Wells had friends. Wells said he would, but then an opportunity beckoned: he accepted an offer to be editorial director of a paper called the *New York Star*. And he asked Kelly to come with him as art director of the new paper. *Animal Comics* had ceased publication a few months before, leaving a small hole to be filled in Kelly's freelancing life, so he went with Wells, becoming the *Star*'s art director with the first issue, June 23, 1948.

The *New York Star* was what was left of a journalist's beatific pipedream. When it folded after a meteoric seven-month run, *The New Yorker* said of it that it had been the "semi-official outlet of advanced liberal thought" put out by "a staff of indefatigable crusaders." The *Star* was actually the continuation of another newspaper, an even more nobly inspired production. Called *PM*, it had been founded by Ralph Ingersoll, an energetic, talented, and successful journalist with an uplifting notion: he wanted to publish an uncompromis-

ing daily newspaper in New York City. The paper would publish the truth — and only the truth (as its staff perceived it) — without political preconceptions. And it would crusade for this truth in its news columns as well as on its editorial pages. To be free to pursue only the dictates of conscience and fact, the paper would take no advertising so it would be beholden to no outside interest. It would pay its way entirely through newsstand sales and subscriptions. It was every newspaperman's dream — to write the truth as he saw it, unencumbered by political or economic considerations.

Ingersoll launched his noble experiment June 18, 1940, with the financial backing of eighteen investors, wealthy idealists all — including Marshall Field III, who was soon the key figure in the enterprise. By September, the paper was losing money so steadily that most of the investors wanted out. Field, who had seen what politcal bias can do to reporting the news in his hometown's *Chicago Tribune*, thought Ingersoll's noble idea needed more time. He bought out the other investors for twenty cents on the dollar, becoming *PM*'s sole financial support. He had every right to assert himself in the conduct of reporting and editorializing in the paper, but he respected Ingersoll's idea and left the idealistic editor to his own devices. But he had been smitten by Ingersoll's high-minded credo, so he went off to do battle with Colonel McCormick's opinion-laden *Tribune* by founding a rival for it, the *Chicago Sun*. The people of Chicago, he vowed, would now have a way to get to the unvarnished facts of the day's events.

Meanwhile, Ingersoll plunged ahead, deeper and deeper into the red. Throughout its eight-year run, *PM* relied on Field's purse; it never ran in the black. Toward the end, it even accepted advertising. But by then, it was too late. By the spring of 1948, Field needed his money for his own paper; he sold his interest to Bartley Crum and Joseph Barnes, who became publisher and editor of the paper. *PM* promptly went on hiatus to be resurrected a month later as the *New York Star*.

The *Star* continued to be an independent voice in

New York's ferociously competitive newspaper market, but it followed a somewhat more conventional path than *PM* had. In the *Star*, opinions were kept out of the news columns and confined to the editorial pages. And it accepted advertising. Otherwise, it was fiercely different from other papers on the newsstand. It was pro-labor, pro-Israel, and pro-Truman in the 1948 Presidential Election campiagn. In other words, its liberal voice championed humanistic values. And Kelly felt at home there.

As art director, Kelly was most of the art department. He drew whatever illustrative matter the paper needed — daily weather "ears," decorative borders, spot drawings for columns, and the like. He was also the *Star*'s political cartoonist, and he had plenty to choose from in selecting his daily targets.

Harry S Truman, the little man from Missouri who had inherited the White House four years previously when Franklin D. Roosevelt died just two months into his fourth term, was the Democrats' nominee by default: none of the party's power brokers had wanted Truman as their candidate, but they couldn't deny the incumbent an opportunity to be elected President on his own if he wanted the chance. And Truman wanted the chance. He was running against Thomas E. Dewey, the governor of New York who had made a name for himself as a racket-busting district attoreny. Two more different personalities could scarcely have been imagined: down-to-earth and matter-of-fact, Truman seemed a country hick in comparison to the suave, reserved (and, unfortunately, stiff and formal) Dewey. All the experts had Dewey pegged as the winner months before either party had chosen a candidate. But the feisty Missourian turned the tables on the experts.

While Dewey, complacent about his eventual victory, made occasional dignified addresses at formal occasions in a few large cities around the country, Truman took a train from coast to coast and border to border, stopping at every town and hamlet en route to make a few remarks from the rear platform of the train. Speaking in a high-pitched Missouri twang, Truman castigated the Republican-controlled Congress for doing nothing to achieve the party's political agenda as it had been announced in the Republican platform. The political experts scoffed at Truman's "whistle-stop" campaign, but the people Truman was talking to were listening. And when Election Day came, they voted for him. By 4 a.m. Wednesday, November 3, it was clear that the underdog had won; Dewey — the unbeatable Dewey — had been beaten. It was the political upset of the century. And Kelly and the *Star* rejoiced.

On the international scene, the historic Berlin airlift was concurrent with the *Star*'s life. In June, the Soviets has closed the corridor to Berlin — the highway and railroad access to the city from West Germany — seeking by siege to thwart the post-war economic recovery that they feared. The United States and its allies were determined that Russian dictator Joseph Stalin would not get what he wanted. They resolved to feed and supply 2.5 million besieged Berliners by air. This unprecedented effort would require round-the-clock operation of a fleet of cargo planes. The airlift began in June, and for many weeks, it couldn't manage to land enough goods to do the job; but by late fall, giant transport planes were taking off and landing every two minutes or so, bringing 4,000 tons into Berlin every day — enough to keep Berliners alive. It was a humanitarian and political triumph of modern ingenuity and brute technology. Joe Stalin had lost. But the episode established him as the world's new villain, replacing Adolf Hitler.

Kelly's political cartoons dealt often with the plight of liberal causes and with Stalin and Truman and Dewey. His cartoons were typical of the style of editorial cartoons of the day: seldom humorous, they were somber pronouncements, trenchant graphic sermons speaking in grim visual metaphors. Powerful enough by the standards of the time, they were scarcely brilliant. They were entirely competent, journeyman efforts — and given Kelly's inexperience at the genre, that is no faint praise. And there was more than a little intimation of what was to come in his work of the period: whenever he depicted the stiff and calculating Dewey, he drew him as some sort of a machine, a mechanical man. (The New York Newspaper Guild, a struggling journalists' union, liked Kelly's work very much: it conferred upon him the Heywood Broun Award for his coverage of the Presidential contest.)

The *Star*'s requirements for cartoons and other art work were not sufficient to consume all of Kelly's time. Nor was the job lucrative enough to enable him to abandon his numerous other endeavors, writing and drawing countless piece-work assignments that he'd become expert at ferreting out. He was a dervish of creative energy in those days, and he always seemed to be working at full capacity. He arrived at the *Star*'s offices in lower Manhattan at 164 Duane Street near City Hall at 11 a.m. and left at 5 p.m. (sometimes stopping for drink and conviviality at Zakely's, a nearby watering hole frequented by the paper's denizens). Before and after his stint at the *Star*, Kelly wrote and drew for his freelance clients.

John Horn (whom Kelly had hired as an assistant because the *Argosy* had laid him off) worked closely with Kelly in those days, and he recorded this incident, indicative of the cartoonist's working habits:

> One day, after finishing the political cartoon of the day, he was about to relax for a moment when he remembered he had another deadline. He turned from his drawing board to his typewriter and began pounding away. He asked me to ring for a messenger. I looked over his shoulder as he was finishing some two and a half pages of copy (in about two minutes). It was a fantasy of the natural world, a children's story of action with a beginning, middle, and end. He had a contract, he told me, to write such stories to be printed on cereal boxes and he hated to give it up.

The *Star*'s management knew that they had a treasure in Kelly's versatility and fecundity: they had raised his salary to that of a top editor after but a couple of weeks. And they listened to what he said. Horn was impressed by how much power and influence his friend had. Kelly once asked him for suggestions about improving the paper; and the ideas Kelly had liked were put into effect immediately.

In late September, Kelly decided that the *Star* needed another comic strip. The paper was running *Little Pedro* by William de la Terre and Crockett Johnson's *Barnaby* (now drawn by Jack Morley), strips it had inherited from *PM*. But Kelly wanted to do one of his own. So art director Kelly directed cartoonist Kelly to produce a new comic strip. And cartoonist Kelly resurrected the swampland characters he'd been drawing for *Animal Comics* until the magazine's demise the year before. Pogo made his newspaper debut on October 4, 1948.

The strip accompanied the *Star* through the remaining weeks of its fated life, ceasing with the paper's last issue on January 28, 1949. But *Pogo*'s brief four-month run had been enough to convince Kelly that this was what he wanted to do. He wanted draw a daily comic strip. For the next several weeks, he made the rounds of the feature syndicate offices in Manhattan, peddling his brain-children. Most syndicates looked down their noses at a "funny animal strip," but at Post-Hall, Robert Hall decided to take a chance. Hall was a little more adventurous than most syndicate chiefs: he would later gamble (and win) with such an unlikely prospect as a strip featuring a Cockney ne'er-do-well barfly and philandering husband named Andy Capp. *Pogo* looked worth a gamble. And so the unassuming possum began his syndicated life on May 16, 1949.

A few pages farther into this volume, you'll find the first *Pogo* strips, the entire *Star* run. And after that, the first six weeks of the syndicated run of the strip. For Kelly fans — and for scholars and critics of the medium — the juxtaposition of these two incarnations provides the opportunity for a fascinating comparison.

Although at first glance the syndicated *Pogo* does not appear much different than the *Star* version, a slightly more prolonged scrutiny reveals that Kelly's graphic style had matured somewhat between October 1948 and May 1949. His lines were a bit bolder, his hatching more strategically deployed, and his figures filled the panels better. And some of his characters were slightly more streamlined in the spring than they had been in the fall. Pogo's nose, for instance, had been shortened a bit, making him a little less top-heavy. But these kinds of variations are not particularly revealing: every cartoonist grows and changes as a graphic stylist, and the way he renders his characters changes, too, the rough edges rubbing off with continued use. Comparing the early work of any cartoonist with any of his subsequent work will yield a battery of conclusions like the ones I've just drawn about Kelly.

But in the two versions of *Pogo* before us, we have something much more insightful about Kelly as a cartoonist than samples of his drawing ability at six month intervals. In the syndicated *Pogo*, Kelly used some of the gags and sequences he had used at the *Star*. But he didn't just reprint the strips from the *Star*: he re-drew everything. Every strip. And in re-drawing them all, Kelly revealed hiself as a conscientious and self-critical crafts-man. He knew that he had grown and improved as an artist. And rather then foist off on an unwitting public the work of an earlier phase in his development, he gave them his best — his current work.

Kelly was also developing as a storyteller between October and May. He did not reuse all of the *Star* material, and most of it that he did use again he changed slightly, some of it quite dramatically. By examining the differences between the two versions of encore sequences in the strip, we can see Kelly assuming greater command of the medium.

In the opening sequence in both versions of the strip, for instance, Kelly toys with the delicate matter of canni-balism. In a strip starring anthropomorphic animals and insects, the role of the humble earthworm on a fishing expedition is more than a little ambiguous. And what do the fish have to say? Philosophically, Kelly would resolve the issue in an exchange between Porkypine

and Rackety-coon Child on November 3, 1949 (11-3), but he would return to the situation again and again throughout the run of the strip. It could scarcely be avoided, and Kelly found it fertile ground for cultivating comedy.

My reason for mentioning this sequence here, how-ever, is to draw attention to the change that Kelly made when he repeated it in May: Churchy LaFemme now gets many of the lines Kelly had given to Pogo in Octo-ber. It's Churchy, not Pogo, who proposes that the worm take employment as fish bait. The change reveals how Kelly now perceived Pogo's personality. By the spring of 1949, the cartoonist had lived with his characters every day for four months. The daily proximity was much more intense than the nodding acquaintance he experi-enced when working with them on a bi-monthly basis for *Animal Comics*. Consequently, he knew them better in May than he had known them in October. And by May, Pogo had become in Kelly's mind too mild-mannered, too kindly a presence in the strip to even think of put-ting a worm on a hook. (And later, when he actually hooks a fish, he's easily intimidated by Champeen Hosshead the Catfish into setting the finny creature free — entirely in character.) Knowing this about Pogo, Kelly made Churchy the heavy in this sequence, thereby affirming at the onset of the strip the essentially benign personality of his leading player.

In the same inaugural sequence, Kelly refines the gag that develops out of Pogo's being cheated of the pro-duct of his labor. The notion of "fifty percent" lends itself more vividly to dramatization than "five percent of thirty-nine," and Kelly gets two good gags out of it on 5-20: Churchy's "half" of the two-fish harvest is a better half than Pogo's, and then Howland Owl cheats him out of half the remainder. And the next day, Albert plays the part that Kelly gave to Owl in the earlier version. This change, like the other ones I've discussed, is clearly an improvement. It brings Albert onstage much earlier than before, for one thing. And the incident itself — Albert greedily consuming the last vestige of Pogo's

industry in front of the hapless possum — is more illus-trative of the personality of Albert than it is of Owl's. Owl may be clever in a cunning, self-serving way, and he may be self-centered (as Albert is most of the time), but he is not unrelentingly, forever voracious (as Albert is all of the time).

Some of the changes Kelly made in the repeated se-quences are much more subtle than these. But they too demonstrate his growth as a cartoonist. In the third week of the syndicated *Pogo*, for example, Kelly repeat-ed almost exactly the situation he had developed during the sixth and seventh weeks of the *Star* version. The substance is the same, but, as his treatment of the visuals in one strip reveals, Kelly was now more skillful at staging the action to tell his story without narrative bumps and grinds. The strip for June 1 (6-1) is better developed than its counterpart 11-12: we see Albert approaching from the distance in the second panel instead of having him pop out at us suddenly from behind a tree.

On several occasions, Kelly improved upon the *Star* version's gags. In 6-22 and 6-23, for instance, he reworks the material of 12-6 to advantage. Houn'dog's vow to stay with Pogo forever gets a funnier conclusion in 6-22, and by shifting the welcoming-home gag to an install-ment all its own, Kelly gave himself enough room to develop fully the physical comedy of Houn'dog's action. We'll see more of this kind of polishing and refining in the next volume, which reprints the remainder of the 1949 strips.

Conspicuously absent from the first months of the strip is the kind of political satire Kelly would become noted for later. In fact, he takes almost no notice of cur-rent events. In the *Star* version, to be sure, the swamp holds an election for sheriff while the rest of the country is electing a President. And Kelly mentions Truman and Dewey by name. (The fact that the swamp's election ends in a dispute over the results is provocative. Was Kelly setting up this situation in anticipation of Truman's defeat? Did he plan to say something much more pointed had Truman lost? We can't say for sure how far in advance of publication Kelly drew his strips for the *Star*; for syndicate distribution, strips must be drawn four to six weeks in advance, but for publication in just the *Star*, Kelly could probably have worked closer to publication date. My guess is that he drew the strips a week in advance. He had the strips for the week of November 1 done before Election Day on the 2nd. But when Truman emerged the victor in the wee hours of November 3, Kelly probably changed plans for that week's sequence. I think he drew a replacement strip for Saturday the 6th: that strip seems to be tacking away from the direction implied by the preceding strips that week.) His final allusion to the Presidential Election is two weeks afterward: in 11-17, a crow shows up, interrupting the storyline to tweak all the experts who had predicted Truman's defeat and who now had to eat crow.

Apart from these passing comments on the Presidential contest, however, Kelly virtually ignores the news of the day. And the newspapers those days were full of the kind of news that Kelly would later joyfully seize upon as the best material for comedy he could find. The day of the ''organization man,'' the conformist in the grey flannel suit, was just dawning. And the infamous Kinsey Report had been published in early 1948 — telling Americans that they were a good deal more active sexually than their Victorian posturing admitted. But more ominous events were casting shadows across the land in 1949.

In May, Chiang Kai-shek, supposed defender of democracy, left mainland China to take up residence on the island of Formosa; Mao Tse-tung and his communist followers now controlled the most populous nation on Earth. In late September, the White House would announce the most alarming news of the Cold War: Russia had exploded an atom bomb a few weeks before. The U.S. had lost its nuclear monopoly. Fear began to stalk the land. How could we have lost both China and atomic supremacy to the communists in such short order? The answer was beginning to surface in

the sensational trial of Alger Hiss, a distinguished young Democrat of Rooseveltian mien. Hiss was accused of perjury, but the question was whether or not he had sold state secrets to the communists. His first trial ended with a hung jury in May; his second trial would begin November 17. The verdict would be handed down in January 1950 and would set the stage for the emergence of another of America's grotesque political figures.

In combination, these events would bubble and simmer, creating a redolent stew of sensation and alarm, which, in just a couple short years, would provide Kelly with a noisome feast of targets for political satire. For the moment, however, none of these goings-on found their way into *Pogo*. For the moment, Pogo and his pals were content with being simply ''nature's screechers,'' a happy-go-lucky band of animals imitating people being, well, human. It was, as the evidence of the good stuff at hand amply testifies, about as a good a way as any to begin a quarter century of commentary on the human condition.

The Cast

It is estimated that the cast of *Pogo* numbers in the thousands. If you count all the bugs and beetles, that is. If you don't, the entourage probably consists of only a few hundred. Still, it is one of the largest casts in comic stips. One of those few hundred characters could pop into the continuity at any time, and each of them had distinct personalities. An impressive array.

In an effort to discover just exactly how many characters were in the strip's cast, we're going to begin a roll call, listing in each of the successive volumes of this series the characters introduced in the strips reprinted therein.

Criteria

To be cited in this listing, a character must be named. "Mr." or "Mis" (Kelly's usage; I use "Miz") constitutes a name when coupled with another word—Miz Hop Frog, Mr. Mailman, Mr. Crane. On occasion, un-named characters are listed here—if they play a "significant" part. The un-named Turkey appeared at Thanksgiving; that seems "significant." Most of the numerous insects and worms, however, are not included here even when they have had speaking parts of several days. A few are included, but most are not.

The listing gives the characters' names in order of their appearance, starting with their *New York Star* incarnations. After the *Star* listing, I begin the chronological rollcall for the syndicated strip. Characters that appeared first in the *Star* and then in the syndicated strip are identified in the *Star* listing with an asterisk (*) and a superscript number. The number indicates the order of their appearance in the syndicated strip. The superscript numbers in the syndicated listing incorporate the characters introduced in the syndicate strip into the same numbering system, so by following only the superscript numbers, you can determine the order of appearance of the characters in the syndicated strip. After 24 characters have been introduced in the syndicated strip, all the characters are completely new to the newspaper incarnation of *Pogo*. Those numbered 1-5 appeared in the syndicated strip in that order before any other characters appeared in that version of the strip. They, with the addition of Beauregard Bugleboy the bloodhound, constituted the cast's principals for several years.

Pogo's Cast in the New York Star

In Order of Appearance:

*Pogo[1]

Un-named Turtle (in other words, not Churchy)

Un-named Porcupine (not Porkypine)

*Churchy Lafemme[2]

*Howland Owl[3]

Crane (un-named)

*Miz Rackety Coon[24]

*Rackety Coon Child[20]

*Albert Alligator[4]

*Lady Bug[15]

*Porkypine[5]

"Secret Weapon" Jones (a skunk)

Widow Woman Bird

*Chug Chug Curtis the Mailman[13] (when he appears in the syndicated strip, he is called "Mr. Mailman" first, then finally, simply "Curtis")

*Miz Hop Frog[8]

*Frog Child[9]

Caw Caw the Crow

*Ol' Hardback the Turtle (named but does not appear)[10]

*Handsome Sam the Turtle[11] (called "Handsome" only in the *Star* version)

Turkey (for Thanksgiving)

*Beauregard Bugleboy the bloodhound (also called Houn'dog)[12] (Beauregard is the only character who appears and fills a substantial role for days—weeks—before he is named. In the *Star*, he appears on December 5 but isn't named until December 15. Kelly used the same basic situation in the syndicated version of the strip. But he embellished the situation more so it took longer to get to Houn'dog's name: he appeared June 21 and wasn't given a name until July 18. Even then, he was called only "Beauregard"—his last name wasn't given in the strip at all in 1949.)

Deacon Mantis McNulty

*Boll Weevil[15]

Orville the Scrooch Owl (screech owl)

Pogo Characters Added in 1949 in the Syndicated Strip

New Characters in Order of Appearance (for Overall Order of Appearance, Including Characters Previously Introduced, Follow Superscript numbers):

Mister Crane[6]

Mister Mailman[7] (probably Chug Chug Curtis; at his next appearance, #13, he's called simply "Curtis")

OCT 4, 1948

OCT 5, 1948

POGO

by Walt Kelly

OCT 6, 1948

WHEN YOU PORKYPINES WANTS TO HUG YOU CHILDREN — HOW YOU MANAGES IT ?

DON'T HUG

DON'T LIKE ANYBODY GOOD ENOUGH TO HUG 'EM

DO YOU EVER ROLL OVER IN BED AN' STICK YO' OWN SELF?

YES AN' I'M *GLAD!* SERVES ME RIGHT!

DON'T LIKE *ANYBODY*

OCT 7, 1948

WHY SO GLUM POGO POSSUM?

H'LO CAP'N CHURCHY LAFEMME I CAN'T FIND NO CATFISH BAIT

COME ON IN YOUR HOUSE, GOT ANY BREAD?

MADE HER THIS MORNING

SQUEEZEY ROLL OUT SOME MORE BREAD BALL BAIT — THEN YOU AN' ME IS EQUAL PARTNERS IN YOUR FISHIN' BUSINESS

BUT THIS IS *MY* BREAD

JUST FOR THAT YOU KEEPS A COOL FIVE PER CENT OF THE FISH THAT BAIT IS MADE OF YOUR BREAD AND *MY BRAINS*

YASSIR! IT ALL SOLID DOUGH

CITY OF NASHVILLE

POGO

by Walt Kelly

OCT 8, 1948

Panel 1: THAT'S THIRTY-NINE FISHES YOU IS CAUGHT — SO HOW YOU LIKES TO HEAR A POEM, POGO? / CRUNCH HER OUT, CHURCHY

Panel 2: "OH BY THE BAYOU BY YOU SIDE I WILL BUY YOU A BY-YOO-TIFFLE BOUQUET, MAME." / MAME? WHAT SHE DOIN' IN THERE?

Panel 3: LET'S US LEAVE MAME'S NAME OUT OF THIS HERE! / I WILL LEAVE BOTH OF YOU OUT--- YOU IS SCARE THE CAT-FISHES

Panel 4: I'M NOT GONE LET OL' MAME BE INSULT FORE AN' AFT---- --GOOD DAY! 36-37-38-39 RIGHT / PERCHANCE I WAS HASTY

OCT 10, 1948

Panel 1: DON'T SEEM LIKE OL' TURTLE LEFT ME MY FAIR SHARE

Panel 2: H'LO POGO POSSUM / HOWLAND OWL, YOU'RE A SCIENTIST IS THIS HERE FISH FIVE PER CENT OF THIRTY-NINE?

Panel 3: MM— I LEFT MY SLIDE RULE IN MY SUNDAY PANTS ----LESSEE---HEY, IS YOU FIVE PER CENT?

Panel 4: HE DON'T SAY— BUT MY PROFESSIONAL SUSPICION IS HE'S A LI'L SKIMPY / A SKIMPY? ALL THE TIME I FIGURES HE'S A CATFISH!

3

OCT 11, 1948

OCT 12, 1948

4

POGO

by Walt Kelly

OCT 13, 1948

HOWDY, MIS' RACKETY COON, WASHIN'?

WASHIN'

MIS' RACKETY COON

THAT REMIND ME — DO RACKETY COONS ALWAYS WASH FOOD 'FORE THEY EATS?

ALWAYS.

WASH 'EM FIRST — THEN EAT 'EM HUH?

YUH-HUH

POPPA!

OCT 14, 1948

YES, POGO, US LI'L OL' RACKETY COONS IS THE CLEANEST LI'L OL' CRITTURS IN THE LI'L OL' SWAMP.

ALWAYS WASH THINGS AFORE WE EATS 'EM FOR EXAMPLE.

EVERY OL' TIME?

EVERY SINGLE LI'L OL' TIME

GLUMP

TAKES THE OL' TASTE OUT --- SORTA ---- DON'T IT?

OH — I DON'T KNOW —— (Now where's Pa's other sock?)

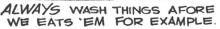

5

OCT 15, 1948

MAN, SHE FEEL LIKE THEY IS BUTTERFLIES IN MY CELLAR.

ALBERT ALLIGATOR

YOU DO LOOK SORT OF PUNY.

POKE 'ROUND, POGO, SEE WHAT IS IT.

NO TRICKS NOW.

BLINK MY PERTY BROWN EYES! A REGULATION BUTTERFLY!

YOU WAS SLEEPIN' WITH YOUR MOUTH OPEN.

THAT OL' SIEVE SHOULD FIX HER. I WAS SUCKED IN BY THE DOWN DRAFT.

HOW I LOOK, POGO?

OCT 17, 1948

YOU SAVED MY LIFE, POGO. I WILL STICK WITH YOU.

BUT YOU MAKES ME LOOK LIKE A GAL WITH A RIBBON BOW.

10-17

OH — YOO-HOO

SUDDENLY I DESPISES OWLS AND TURTLES

HELLO HONEY, WHAT'S YOUR NAME? I'M A LADY BUG, NAME OF LOU. WE SHOULD GET TOGETHER AND TALK.

THAT'S THE LAST STRAW! EVERYBODY OFF — EVERYBODY OFF — BEFORE THIS LADY FORGETS SHE'S A GENTLEMAN.

POGO

by Walt Kelly

OCT 18, 1948

OCT 19, 1948

OCT 20, 1948

YOUR FRIEND, POGO, TOLD ME THAT I GONE BE A BOBOLINK NEXT

ONCE I IS A CATERPILLAR. THEN I IS A COCOON — NOW I IS A BUTTERFLY

NEXT YOU GONE BE A BOBOLINK?

OH, I IS. — AND MIGHTY PROUD TO BE IT.

BOBOLINK TURNOVERS WITH POT LICKER IS MY FAVORITE

GET FAT, NOW.

PHOOEY ON THIS STRIP, I GONE ASK FOR A TRANSFER TO LI'L PEDRO.

OCT 21, 1948

HELP! HELP! POLICE, POLICE, POLICE, POLICE! A DANGEROUS CHARACTER IS LOOSE IN THE SWAMPLAN'

WHO IT BE PORKYPINE?

PERSON NAME OF PORKYPINE TO WIT, ME.

YOU —? DANGEROUS? HAW HAW!

YASSERREE, US NEEDS PROTECTION FROM LI'L OL' ME. HELP, POLICE. HELP!

PORK BOY, YOU KILLS ME — HEE HOO!

OUCH! YOU IS A BRAMBLEY OL' THING!

SEE WHAT I MEANS? I JUS SAT ON MY OWN TAIL — POLICE POLICE. HELP.

8

POGO

by Walt Kelly

OCT 22, 1948

OL' PORKYPINE CLAIM WE NEEDS A POLICE FORCE — SO NATURAL *I* WILL BE THE BOSS.

What!?

THE BEST MAN IS WHAT WE NEEDS — WE'LL PICK THE BEST MARKSMAN 'MONGST OUR MIDST.

OKAY — THE BEST MARKSMAN IS ME — NEED ANY PROOF?

YOWP!

ANY MARKSMAN CONTEST GOTTA INCLUDE OL' FRIENDLY ME, CHILDREN.

IT'S "SECRET WEAPON" JONES

OCT 24, 1948

I LEAVES IT TO YOU. OL' SECRET WEAPON JONE IS NOBODY TO MESS WITH IN A TARGET SHOOTIN' MATCH.

THEN WE PICKS OUR SHERIFF BY A NATURAL BORN EE-LECTION

LONG AS US GOTTA RESORT TO DEMOCRACY LET ME REFER TO A CANDIDATE WHAT STAND OUT — MAN WHAT CAN'T BE BEAT!

WHO HE?

FRIENDLY OL' ME. THAT'S WHO!

WOOP?

I IS A PITIFUL WIDOW WOMAN LOOKIN' FOR A HOME SO DON'T GO SWALLOWIN' MUCH — IT COZY-KINDA IN HERE.

ALBERT GIVIN' SHELTER TO A WIDOW WOMAN

GOOD

9

OCT 25, 1948

ALBERT, LONG AS YOU GOT THAT WIDOW WOMAN BIRD IN YO' MOUTH, YOU CAN'T TALK LESSEN YOU EVICTS THE GAL.

MMF.

AN' IF YOU EVICTS HER YOU IS MAKIN' IT HARD FOR A PITIFUL CRITTUR...... AN' I WILL BE EE-LECTED SHERIFF 'CAUSE US ISN'T WANT ANY HARD-HEARTED PUBLIC SERVANTS.

FELLOW VOTERS, HOW CAN YOU STAND IDLE BY AN' WATCH OL' ALBERT BEIN' CRUEL TO A WIDOW WOMAN?

I IS NOT!

YOU IS DID IT! HOW CRUEL!

CAST ON THE CURB WITH MY FURNITURE AN' STARVIN' BABIES.

I FORGET SHE WAS IN RESIDENCE.

OCT 26, 1948

OH, WHAT IS HAPPEN TO THE OL' HOSPITALITY OF THE LAND OF HUMMOCK AND TUSSOCK? OL' ALBERT FLINGED THE WIDOW WOMAN OUTEN HER SNUG LI'L HOME.

YOU IS A BUNCH OF LI'L FAKERS HER HOME WAS IN MY NATURAL BORN MOUTH — AN' IT WAS MINE FIRST —— BUT I WILL RESTORE THE WIDOW WOMAN — NEEDIN' YOUR VOTES AS I DOES.

GOODY, I IS A OBJECK OF PITY.

SHE POPS OUT ANYWAYS WHILE I WAS A-HOOTIN'— BESIDES SHE GUM UP THE TRAFFIC — DON'T FORGIT I GITTIN' HONGRY.

HONGRY? DON'T YOU DARE — YOU CANNIBAL YOU — FOR SHAME! FOR SHAME! FIE!

YES, FIE.

WHAT'D I DO NOW?

10

POGO

by Walt Kelly

OCT 27, 1948

OL' ALBERT PROMISES NOT TO SWALLOW ME — SO I DO BELIEVE I'LL ROOST IN HERE FOR A SPELL.

FUMPH!

HE CAN'T EVICT A WIDOW WOMAN.

HERE'S SOME STICKS AND TWINE AND LEAVES TO BUILD YOU A NEST WITH, MIS WIDOW WOMAN!

GOODY

SINCE YOU BEIN' SO HOSPITABLE, ALBERT, GO AHEAD AN' GIVE A CAMPAIGN SPEECH FOR SHERIFF — WE IS A FRIENDLY AUDIENCE NOW

THAT'S FAIR, POGO

MOOMFA WUMPA GOOBOGGA WUPP! BMPFF ZKOPL!

HE NOT VERY CLEAR ON A FEW POINTS THERE

HE IMPOLITE SPEECHIN' WITH HIS MOUTH FULL

WK

OCT 28, 1948

EVER SINCE YOU PACKS THEM CUTE CATFISH SAN'WICHES HOWLAND OWL, I IS BEEN CRAZY IN FAVOR OF YOU FOR SHERIFF.

CHURCHY LA FEMME I APPOINTS YOU MY NATURAL BORN CAMPAIGN MANAGER —— US WILL BEAT OUT OL' ALBERT AN' POGO.

US WILL CHUNK THE RASCALS OUT — YOU GONE WHUP THE OPPOSITION LIKE THEY IS OL' TILLY BIRDS.

HUZZAH!

OH WIGGLE! BUT I IS PROUD — WHAT MUST I DO FIRST?

START VOTIN'! MY SAKES, IF YOU VOTES STEADY FROM NOW ON WE IS A SHOO IN!

WALT KELLY

11

POGO

by Walt Kelly

OCT 29, 1948

OCT 31, 1948

12

POGO
by Walt Kelly

NOV 1, 1948

THAT'S RIGHT, FELLOW CRITTURS, STEP UP AN' CAST YOUR VOTES INTO THE HAT — WE ELECTIN' A SHERIFF.

FOOF ON YOUR EE-LECTIN'S NOBODY LET ME CAMPAIGN — STUFF MY MOUTH UP WITH A OL' BIRD NEST

YOUR HOT SEEGAR ASHES COTCHED THE VOTES ON FIRE

YOWP

EVERY VOTE BURN TO A CRISP EXCEPT ONE — WHAT SHE SAY?

IT SAY P-O-G-O THAT SPELL OWL — OWL IS THE WINNER! HOT DOG!

NOV 2, 1948

P-O-G-O SPELLS ME! I IS THE WINNER — NOT YOU!

PERCHANCE YOU QUESTION MY PROFESSIONAL AMBIGUITY?

POGO, NOBODY CAN SPELL 'CEPT YOU AND OWL — IT'S YOUR WORD BE GAINST HE.

I IS BEIN' FLIMMED AND FLAMMED.

♫ Hmmmm

POGO, YOU IS RIGHT, THIS VOTE IS YOURS..

OH, JES' GOODY FOR ME!

HOWEVER, THAT LOVIN' UPSTATE VOTE IS JES' COMIN' IN.

AND BEHOLE! IT SAY S-I-Z-E, (THAT SPELL OWL) — SIX AND SEVEN-EIGHTHS —— THE LATE UPSTATE VOTE COUNT SHOW OL' OWL IS WINNER BY A NATURAL BORN LANDSLIDE!

SIZE 6⅞

13

NOV 3, 1948

NOV 4, 1948

by Walt Kelly

NOV 8, 1948

NOV 9, 1948

NOV 10, 1948

NOV 11, 1948

17

POGO

by Walt Kelly

NOV 15, 1948

HEY, WORM! ALBERT SWALLOWED THE FROG CHILD BY MISTAKE — HOW YOU LIKES THE JOB OF GOIN' INSIDE AND RESCUIN' THE BOY?

HOO HEE — STOP WIGGLIN' IN THERE.

YASSIR, BY ACCIDENT I SWALLOWS THAT OL' POLLYWOG.

PEOPLE DON'T SWALLOW OTHER PEOPLE BY MISTAKE!

AAAH, I WOULDN'T LET YOU IN ANYWAYS.

FAUGH!

THERE GO THE ONLY BARITONE WORM IN GOOCHIE COUNTY.

NOV 16, 1948

YOU GOIN' DOWN AFTER THAT LI'L OL' POLLYWOG BOY I SWALLOWED BY ACCIDENT?

YASSERREE, I GONE TAKE THE PLUNGE

WHAT'S THE CANDLE FOR?

WHY, MAN, IT DARKER NOR A COAL BUCKET DOWN THERE.

'FORE YOU GOES, POGO, LET'S JUS' SHAKE HANDS.

DIDN'T MEAN TO HURT YOUR FEELIN'S.

MUST BE ANOTHER WAY TO ROUSE OUT THAT FROG CHILD.

19

NOV 17, 1948

NOV 18, 1948

POGO

by Walt Kelly

NOV 19, 1948

HELLO OL' PORKYPINE. WE IS TAKEN CARE OF A OL' TADPOLE BOY.

HOW SHARPER THAN A SERPENT'S TOOTH IT IS TO HAVE A THANKLESS CHILD.

LOOK NOT AGHAST--- I, TOO, AM A BABY SITTER!

BUT REVILED, COMPLAINED AGAINST AND SLANDERED BY MY CLIENTELE --- AH, SLANDER, WHOSE STING IS SHARPER THAN THE SWORD.

YOU IS MORE OR LESS POINTY YOUR OWN SELF.

BUT COME, MY BOY, IT'S BACK TO THE MINES.

SIT EASY, MISTER PINE.

LUCKY THING IT'S OL' HARD BACK TURTLES LI'L' BOY HE'S TAKIN' CARE OF.

NOV 21, 1948

YOU CARRY THE FISH POLES, ALBERT, AND I WILL CARRY THE FROG CHILD ON HIS FIRST FISHIN' PARTY.

TAD, I WILL TELL YOU BEDTIME STORY WHAT GONE TEACH YOU A LESSON --- ONCE UPON A TIME THEY WAS A LI'L' OL' SHIRT-TAIL POLLYWOG AN' A HORRIBOBBLE ALLIGATOR COME SWIMMIN' BY----

THE 'GATOR OPEN UP HIS OL' FIERCE JAWBONES WIDE AND HE GO 'ROWGER-ROWGER WOGGA-BOGGA-SNAP!

YEOW! YOU IS SCARE ME!

LOOK OUT! YOU SPILLIN' THE OL' POLLYWOG!

21

POGO

by Walt Kelly

NOV 22, 1948

MAN ALIVE, WE LOST THE LI'L' OL' POLLYWOG BOY!

MIS' HOP FROG GONE CARRY ON SOMETHIN' FIERCE.

HOO BOY! HERE SHE COME! GROSP UP SOME NATURAL BORN SWAMP WATER.

WE MUDDIES UP THE WATER SO'S THE CUTE LI'L OL' SHIRT TAIL TAD WOULD SLEEP BEST IN THE DARK.

WHO FLUNG THE GOO?

MY CHILD!

NOV 23, 1948

COME HOME AN' GIT WASHED!

BUT, I'M *NOT* YOUR LITTLE BOY! I'M A NATURAL BORN TURTLE BY TRADE.... HANDSOME SAM, THE TURTLE.

POOR SAM.

POOR MIS HOP FROG.

WE GOTTA FIND THAT LI'L LOST OL' SHIRT-TAIL POLLY-WOG --- GIVE A HOLLER FOR THE CRITTUR UNDERNEATH OF THE WATER THERE, POGO.

FOOF! MY HOLLER BACK-FIRE AND THE OL' SWAMP RUSH IN FIT TO KILL --- I IS PRACTICAL *IN-UN*DATED.

22

NOV 26, 1948

POGO

by Walt Kelly

NOV 28, 1948

NOV 29, 1948

24

DEC 2, 1948

UNFAIR, UNFAIR, UNFAIR!

HUSH YOUR YAWPIN', POGO; YOU 'S SPOIL MY WRITIN'.

BUT OL' OWL CLAIM WE CAN'T BE IN THE MIAMI BEACH CONTES' CAUSE WE IS EMPLOYES OF THE STAR.

NO!

OH GALL! GALL! BITTER, BITTER WORMWOOD! MY MAIDEN LITERARY EFFORT GONE TO NAUGHT ON A ONE WAY TICKET.

AW, SHECKS! READ ME YOUR LETTER— I WILL WHISTLE AND STOMP MY FEETS.

READ IT? MAN, HOW MANY TALENTS YOU EXPECT IS WROP UP IN ONE BOY? I ONLY GOOD AT WRITIN'— NEVER GIVES A HOOT FOR READIN' WHAT I WRITES

DEC 3, 1948

LOOK LIKE A HARD LI'L' OL' WINTER.

INDEED IT DO.

THAT WAY— THAT WAY! EVER'BODY WENT THAT WAY.

GITS COLD HERE'BOUTS —·· THIS IS ICEBERG COUNTRY.

CAN'T WATCH THEM MIGRATIN' FLEAS TOO CLOSE ON THEIR WAY FROM NORTHERN FEEDIN' GROUNDS.

THEY IS CUTE, BUT TOO MUCH ON THE BITEY SIDE.

POGO

by *Walt Kelly*

DEC 5, 1948

HELP, HELP, HELP, HELP, HELP, HELP, HELP, HELP, ROOTER BAGGER ROOTER BAGGER, HELP, HELP, HELP.

DOES YOU GOT TIME, MAN YONDER SEEM TO HAVE A PRESSIN' NEED FOR HELP.

DO HE?

WHAT ALL THE FUSS, HOUN' DOG?

I'M TRAPPED! CAUGHT! ENSNARED IN SOME FIENDISH **DEE**-VICE OF THE HUNTSMAN. **OH** HELP, I SAY, HELP INDEED.

LIFT UP YOUR NATURAL BORN FOOT.

SAVED! SAVED! **REE**-LEASED! FREE ONCE MORE TO ROAM. JOY-JOY INDEED.

DEC 6, 1948

SMUSH! THERE'S A KISS FOR YOU. PART OF A GENERAL SERVICE OF DEVOTION **AND** LOVE PERFORMED DAILY BY MAN'S BEST FRIEND, TO WIT, THE DOG.

GO AWAY TO WIT.

YOU SAVED MY LIFE YESTERDAY, SIR! BULLY, SIRRAH, BULLY FOR YOU. BULLY, BULLY INDEED. *NEVER* SHALL I LEAVE YOU.

WHAT'S SO NATURAL BORN BULLY 'BOUT THAT?

LET US SUPPOSE THAT YOU ARE COMING HOME AFTER A HARD DAY'S WORK.

KIND OF A STRAIN ON MY S'POSER

WITHOUT A LOVING DOG-YOU WOULD FACE AN EMPTY DOOR—BUT BEHOLD HOW A DOG SPRUCES UP THE HOME-COMING. **WELCOME!**

WAHOO! WELCOME, WELCOME!

HELP!

DEC 7, 1948

DO YOU *HAVE* TO BE SO FAITHFUL *AND* TRUB --- NIGHT AND DAY--? YOUR DEVOTED SNORIN' ROCKS THE BED.

DOG IS MAN'S BEST FRIEND, SIR~ ~*EV*·ER LOVING.

IF YOU DO NOT ENJOY HAVING ME WATCH BENEATH THE BED ~ I SHALL TAKE UP MY VIGIL HERE.

OWP.

SURELY YOU HAVE ROOM IN YOUR HEART FOR THE TRUE FRIEND OF MAN?

HEART GOT A PLENTY ROOM.

IT'S THE *HOUSE* WHAT ISN'T GOT ROOM ENOUGH FOR A MESS OF *EV·ER* LOVIN' *AND* DAUNTLESS FRIENDS AND *REE*·LATIONS.

DEC 8, 1948

PERSONAL, I ISN'T FOND OF HOUN'DOGS USUAL — THEY WHOP ROUN' HOOTIN' AN' HOLLERIN' ---SCARIN' THE SWAMP CRITTURS AN' A-CARRYIN' ON SHAMEFUL.

BUT I'M NOT ONE WHO PURSUES GAME. —AH, **NO** ~ THIS FRIEND OF MAN IS A SPECIALIST, ONE WHO LOOKS FOR LOST OR STRAYED INDIVIDUALS.

AYE, SIRRAH ---WE BLOODHOUNDS ARE SURE FOOTED AND KEEN OF NOSE— —MENTALLY FIT –PHYSICALLY ALERT WE *ALWAYS* FIND OUR MAN.

WHAT YOU DOIN' HERE? NOBODY LOST HERE.

I BEG TO DIFFER.

WHO LOST?

ME.

DEC 9, 1948

HOUN'DOG, THIS IS OL' PORKYPINE. PORK BOY SAY HE DON'T LIKE **NO** BODY.

JUST THE OPPOSITE OF MAN'S BEST FRIEND, THE DOG, WHO IS TRULY A LOVING, KINDLY SOUL.

PORKY PINE

UMPH

OVERCOME WITH MODESTY~~I **BLUSH** TO THINK OF THE VIRTUES SHARED BY MY KIND.

HE CARRY ON LIKE THAT CONSTANT.

WHAT KIND OF VIRTUES IS THESE WHAT MAKE A KID RASH OUT IN BLUSHES?

MY FAVORITE HATE IS THE CRITTUR WHAT STUCK ON HIMSELF - I DON'T LIKE **ME** WHEN **I** DO IT, AND IF I DON'T LIKE OL' FAVORITE ME, I'M NOT GONE LAY WAKE NIGHTS THINKIN' 'BOUT **ANYBODY ELSE.**

THE DOG LISTENS WITH GREAT COURTESY AND A SAD FOREBEARANCE

DEC 10, 1948

YOU NOTHIN' BUT A LOST HOUN'DOG SO STOP PUTTIN' ON A BRAG.

AHEM, MAN'S BEST FRIEND LOATHES THE UNCOUTH ~ ~HE IS DIGNIFIED, CALM AND REFINED ~~ YET, MARK YOU, SIR, HE IS ALERT ~~ ALERT And A-WARE

INDEED, PERCEPTION IS OUR WATCHWOR~~YEOWP!

KLUNK

YES, AS I WAS SAYING, FORGIVENESS IS OUR WATCHWORD.

IT **WAS** HIGH-TONED OF YOU TO **NOT** STAY MAD AT THE TREE ~~ YOU ONLY BIT IT ONCE.

POGO

by Walt Kelly

DEC 12, 1948

CASE YO' LIL' CRITTURS FORGIT, I IS THE NATURAL BORN SHERIFF OF THIS COUNTY.

BULLY, SIR, JUST BULL-EE FOR YOU.

GOT A SECRET DOCUMENT HERE — IN *MONGOLIAN* I DO BEE-LIEVE.

YOU JUST IS A-HOLDIN' HER ALL UPSIDE DOWN.

IT SAY A PERSON NAME BEAUREGARD BUGLEBOY IS WANTED ··· THIS A POSTER FOR THE PO-LICE.

I DIDN'T KNOW YOU WAS A MONGOLIAN, POGO

I ISN'T

THEN, BY JINGLEBERRY, DON'T GO A-READIN' MONGOLIAN SECRETS WHAT IS STRICTLY PO-LICE BUSINESS.

DEC 13, 1948

ALL YOU DEPUTIES GOTTA REALIZE WE GONE USE OUR WITS — NO SACRIFICE IS TOO GREAT — WE UP AGAINST A TRICKY CRIMINAL.

I WILL STEP BEHIND THIS TREE AND GIVE YOU THE FIRST LESSON IN HOW TO CATCH OL' BEAUREGARD BUGLEBOY, THE FUGITIVE.

DON'T KNOW ME, DO YOU?

IT'S BEAUREGARD!

GIT HIM!

DOG MY CATS! YOU TURNS OUT TO BE ALBERT IN *DIS*-GUISE!

THAT IS MORE OR LESS A DISAPPOINTMENT.

30

POGO

by Walt Kelly

DEC 14, 1948

THE BEST FRIEND THAT MAN EVER HAD, TO WIT: THE DOG, OFFERS HIS SERVICES IN TRACKING DOWN THE CRIMINAL.

QUIET, TO WIT, THE LAW IS A-PONDERIN'

THE KEEN EYE OF THE DOG, EVER WATCHFUL, FASTENS ON A SUSPICIOUS OBJECT.

YOWP! BUGLE BOY IS SNUNK UP AHIND US!

DOG MY CATS! BUGLEBOY IS GOT AWAY---- HE BEAT UP ON MY TAIL BONE TOO.

WORST TASTING FUGITIVE I EVER TACKLED IN A LONG DISTINGUISHED CAREER OF CRIMINOLOGY.

WHERE'S A COP? LOOKY MY HAT!

DEC 15, 1948

SINCE YOU CALLED ME IN TO HELP LOOK FOR BUGLE-BOY, I SUGGEST WE CAPTURE OUR QUARRY

GREAT.

WE'LL SWAP COSTUMES - OUR FUGITIVE WILL BE THROWN OFF HIS GUARD.

YOUR COLLAR IS AWFUL SKIMPY

LET ME FASTEN IT FOR YOU-- --HMMM-- SOMETHING WRITTEN ON IT-- B·U·G·L· WHAT!?

ROWF! YOU'RE UNDER ARREST - YOUR COLLAR HAS BUGLEBOY'S NAME ON IT! YOU, ALBERT, ARE BEAUREGARD BUGLEBOY IN DISGUISE.

NO FOOLIN'?

DEC 16, 1948

DEC 17, 1948

POGO

by Walt Kelly

DEC 19, 1948

JUST TO SHOW THERE'S NO HARD FEELINGS, ALBERT, LET'S SPLIT MY SURPRISE CHRISTMAS GIFT.

I ACCEPTS

LET'S SEB WHAT UNCLE ROWF SENT ME — MERCY! BONES! HOW THOUGHTFUL.

GREAT! I LIKES BONES MOST GOOD AS ARY DOG.

HELP YOURSELF ----- HERE'S A NOTE FROM UNCLE ROWF -- BZZZZ MM - WZR - UMSMUP - WP --- BONES SHOULD LAST A LONG TIME HE SAYS

NOT WITH ME AROUND

THEY'RE MADE OF RUBBER.

DEC 20, 1948

I KNOW IT'S FOUR O'CLOCK IN THE MORNING BUT I THOUGHT I'D DROP BY. CHRISTMAS IS COMING *AGAIN!* IT'S AN EVER PRESENT NUISANCE.

P. Possum

WHAZZAT?

DON'T LIKE *ANYBODY* 'CEPT ONE CRITTUR WHOM I *DISLIKES* LESS THAN MOST-- BEEN SAVING SOMETHING FOR HIM SINCE AUGUST.

A BLUNT INSTRUMENT?

A DAISY - IT'S YOURS! DON'T THANK ME. I HATE FAWNING MAUDLIN SENTIMENT-- YOU DON'T SEE DAISIES THIS TIME OF THE YEAR. I ENJOYED THIS ONE. MAYBE YOU WILL, TOO.

WASTE NOT-WANT NOT ~~~ KEEP IT AND HAVE A MERRY CHRISTMAS~~ IF THE REST OF THE SWAMP CRITTURS DON'T LIKE YOU ANY BETTER THAN I DO, YOU WON'T GET A SIMPLE GOOD MORNING.

Thank you, ol' Porkypine

POGO by Walt Kelly

DEC 21, 1948

DEC 22, 1948

34

DEC 23, 1948

MAN'S LOYAL FRIEND, TO WIT: CANIS FAMILIARIS, HAS PUT IN A HARD DAY ROUNDING UP ORPHANS FOR THE CHRISTMAS PARTY, POGO. — — — UH- COULD YOU GET BY WITHOUT ORPHANS?

WHY?

ONLY ORPHANS AVAILABLE SHOWED UP WITH FOUR AND FIVE MOTHERS OR FATHERS APIECE — — WORD OF THE PARTY GOT ABOUT-- —THERE *IS* ONE BONA FIDE ORPHAN, IF I CAN CATCH HIM.

CATCH HIM?

HE'S THE FUGITIVE TYPE — SEEMS TO BE WELL SUPPORTED HOWEVER — **HOWP! ORROR!** BOBBAROFFA·MUMBER·WOFFER. SMOP! SMOP! SMOP!

WHAT *IN* THE WORLD KIND OF TALK. IS THAT?

FLEA TALK! JUST TOLD HIM (IN FLEA) A PARTY'S COMIN'UP. HE'S A GENUINE ORPHAN.

I DOESN'T TALK FLEA - DOES HE SPEAK SWAMP?

SMOP KABOBBA!

DEC 24, 1948

NOBODY WILL SING CHRISTMAS CAROLS- ALBERT IS MAD AN' WON'T BE SANTY- —CAN'T FIND NO ORPHANS FOR A PARTY —'CEPT ONE LONE FLEA

RELAX... I'LL BE A REINDEER

BIG PARTY HERE

SO YOU, FLEA, GET BUSY AND HAVE A GOOD TIME --- --HOUN' DOG, TELL HIM WHAT TO DO, IN FLEA.

HIST! NOISES FROM THE STOVE!

WOCKA MOCKA DOCKA?

MERRY~ KAYRISSMUS! SOMEBODY PULLS A KNIFE ON ME --YOWP! YOWP-YOWP!

IT OL' ALBERT.

PORK-AND-PINE! HOW YOU GITS IN THERE?

JES' NATURAL SLUM DOWN THE CHIMBLEY. CHRISTMAS GOT A FIERCE TRADITION ON HER· *GOTTA HAVE A SANTY CLAUS.*

MERRI WERRY KRINGLE KRANGLE.

POGO

by Walt Kelly

DEC 28, 1948

DEC 29, 1948

37

JAN 4, 1949

HEY, OL' ALBERT, COME ON OUT FISHIN' — IT TOO NICE A DAY TO WORK YOU FINGERBONES TO THE CORE.

CAN'T.

THE NATCHEZ BELLE

I SPRUCIN' UP MY HOUSE. PUTTIN' UP NEW SIGNS AN' ALL.

ATBER

ATBER? THAT DOESN'T SPELL ALBERT! MAN, YOU CAN'T SPELL YOUR WAY THRU A BOOK OF CIGARETTE PAPERS!

ATBER

IF IT DOESN'T SPELL ALBERT, IT DOESN'T SPELL WELCOME EITHER — ACTUAL IT SAY "42 MILES TO SAVANNAH." SO, GIT GOIN', YOU EDUCATED LI'L SPRAT.

JAN 5, 1949

OL' ALBERT GO SPELLIN' HIS NAME A-T-B-E-R— I FIGURE SHE MORE LIKE THIS HERE.

OUGHT TO GOT A "URR" IN IT SOMEPLACE.

MAN! MR. BOLL WEEVIL, YOU ISN'T KNOW THEM ALFIE BITS LETTERS! WHO EVER HEARD TELL ON THE LETTER, "URR"?

YOU JES' NOW IS HEARD TELL ON IT.

THAT DOES IT! THAT DOUBLE DOG DING DONG DOES IT! WHAT US NEEDS IS A SCHOOL!

HMMPH.

OH, I CAN SEE IT NOW. IVY GROWIN' OVER HALLS AND CHAPEL BELLS KLINKIN' OUT THE HOURS FOR TEA AN' BREAKFIRST.

BULLY! WITH FRIED 'TATERS AN' WHUPPED CREAM!

IVORY GROANIN' OVERALLS?

JAN 6, 1949

IF THIS SCHOOL GONE HAVE A HEAD MAN - **I** IS THE *NATURAL CHOICE* --- **YOU** GONE BE A REG'LAR PUPIL.

YOU?!

FOOEY. I QUITS!

MR. WEEVIL, I POINTS YOU THE TRUAN' OFFICER. FOTCH IN YONDER FUGITIVE.

FAUGH! A NATURAL BORN ACADEMIC TRAVESTY.

PLEASE COME TO SCHOOL, MR. OWL, PLEASE, SIR?

I SCORNS YOU! SCORN! SCORN! SCORN!

HEY! CAREFUL! DOES YOU TROMP A BUG AN' SKOOSH THE BOY, US GITS RAIN. SO, CAREFUL.

STOMP! STOMP! STOMP!

JAN 7, 1949

YOU'LL SPEND THE NEX' SIX YEARS STAYIN' AFTER SCHOOL FOR STOMPIN' AT THE TRUAN' OFFICER.

NOW, POGO, WHAT'S THIS DO-JIGGY WHAT LOOK LIKE A SAW-HORSE?

I GOOD AT THAT LETTER. SHE'S OLD **A**.

ABCDE
12345

NO FOOLIN'?! I MEAN YASSER! WHAT THE NEX' CUTE LI'L OL THING O' MACBOBBLE?

NATURAL, SHE'S A "B".

ABCDE
12345

ANYMORE IMPERTIMENTS FROM YOU, MR. OWL, AN' YOU GONE BE CHONKED OUTEN SCHOOL AND NEVER WILL GET EDUCATED! BEES IS BUGS WITH WINGS - GO FLAPPIN' ROUND SAYIN' BUZZZZZZZZ 'MEMBER THAT NOW.

41

POGO by Walt Kelly

JAN 9, 1949

BEHOLD CLOSE, PUPILS.. THIS HERE THE WAY BEES LOOK - BZZZZZZZZ BZZZZZZZZZZZLLLIIIIIZ

ON THE OTHER HAND, OBSERVE THE DIFFERMINTS BETWEEN BEES AND GRASSHOPPLES... ...GRASSHOPPLES CRUNCH DOWN LOW...

THEN, LIGHT AS A CIPHER, **UP** SPRINGS OL' GRASSHOPPLE..

BLOONK!

GUESS YOU GOT YOUR TEACHIN' JOB BACK, OWL. PROFESSOR ALBERT IS SUFFERED A MENTAL COLLAPSE.

JAN 10, 1949

FIRST THING US DO IN THIS SCHOOL IS TEACH YOU KIDS ALL ABOUT BROTHERLY LOVE.

— AND SISTERLY.

AN' MOTHERLY

FATHERLY

BROTHERLY LOVE IS THE GRADE A NUMBER ONE HOT DOG ITEM IN ALL THE WORL'.. ~YEEOP

FLUG!

HEY. **WHAT HAPPENED** TO THAT OL' BROTHERLY LOVE?

I'LL SETTLE THAT RIGHT NOW~~I IS A OWL - IS YOU A OWL, LI'L' SHIRT TAIL 'TAD?

NOPE. *I* IS A RACKETY COON.

THEN US ISN'T BROTHERS --- -- ROWR!

JAN 11, 1949

JAN 12, 1949

JAN 13, 1949

JAN 14, 1949

JAN 16, 1949

JAN 17, 1949

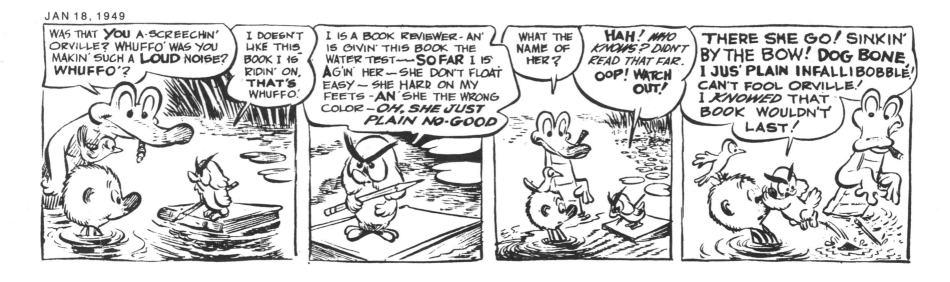

JAN 20, 1949

JAN 21, 1949

POGO

by Walt Kelly

SEEM LIKE LI'L' OL' SCROOCH OWL GOT A PEACHY SYSTEM WHEN HE TEAR EVERY SECOND PAGE OUTEN HIS BOOKS.

IT CERTAINLY DO CUT DOWN THE READIN' HE GOTTA DO.

DIDN'T THE LI'L' SCAPER REVIEW THE BOOK GOOD ENOUGH, TEACHER?

COUSIN ORVILLE FINDS ALL KINDS OF TROUBLE WITH THAT OL' BOOK-- BAD PLOT AND WORSE CHARACTERS AN' A MESS OF BAD SPELLIN' TO BOOT. THEN HE DISCOVER HE BEEN READIN' MISTER WEBSTER'S INTERNATIONAL DICTIONARY.

YOU GOTTA ADMIT THAT TITLE IS NO BALL OF FIRE.

PHOO! I IS TIRED OF ALL THESE LI'L' COMEDIANS KNOCKIN' THEY BRAINS OUT EV'YDAY -- JUS' GONE REE-LAX TODAY.

H'LO POGO 'POSSUM.

WORM *BOY!* I GONE PLAY HOOKEY TODAY AND GO FISHIN' -- COME ON 'LONG.

NOPE -- THE KING OF PATAGONIA IS WAITIN' LUNCH FO' ME --- BESIDES WHEN *YOU* GO FISHIN --

-- I ISN'T TH' BOY WHAT ACHES TO PLAY *HOOKEY* WITH YOU....

NOBODY KNOW THE ANGLES LIKE A FRIENDLY LI'L OL' WIGGLE-WORM.

JAN 27, 1949

JAN 28, 1949

MAY 16, 1949

H'LO, CHURCHY LA FEMME, I'M TAKIN' CARE OF THIS LI'L' OL' BACKWARD CHILD.

THAT'S MIGHTY SOCIABLE, POGO 'POSSUM.

TRYIN' TO TEACH HIM TO GO FORWARD IN LIFE.

WOOP! THERE HE GO! IS THAT BACKWARDS OR FORWARDS?

WAIT! WHICH WAY IS YOU POINTIN'?

IT HARD TO FIGURE THE ANGLES ON A WORM CHILD.

MAY 17, 1949

POGO 'POSSUM, THIS WORM CHILD YOU IS WATCHIN' OUGHT TO LEARN A TRADE.

WHAT PROFESSION YOU GOT IN MIND FO' THE BOY, CAP'N' CHURCHY LA FEMME?

FIRST I COVERS THE LI'L' OL' TAD'S EARS--- --- HOW YOU FIGURE HE LIKES TO WORK AS A OL' FISH BAIT?

OOP! I COVERS THE WRONG END!

NOW HE GONE TELL HIS MA YOU WAS A-USIN' UNCOUTH LANGUAGE.

51

 # POGO
by Walt Kelly

MAY 18, 1949

Panel 1:
I FEARED YOU CAN'T CONVINCE THE WORM CHILD HE OUGHT TO BE FISH BAIT.
BUT LOOKY AT THE OPPORTUNITY, SIR. YOU FIXED FOR LIFE DOES YOU DO IT.

Panel 2:
WHAT FUN! YOU GRABS THE HOOK AN' QUICK DAGS HER AT THE CATFISHES.

Panel 3:
HAW!

Panel 4:
NO FAIR! YOU IS DELIBERATE DONE HURT THE CHILD'S FEELIN'S.

MAY 19, 1949

Panel 1:
DIGGIN' FOR BAITY WORMS IS HARD WORK. SO I WILL WHISTLE UP THE CRITTURS BY BLOWIN' SOME HIGH CLASS MUSIC.

Panel 2:
KEEP YOUR PEEPERS ON THE WORM HOLE, POGO. PRETTY SOON OUT CRAWLS THE LI'L' OL' SCAPERS FASCINATED TO A TURN.

Panel 3:
THERE'S ONE NOW!
YOWP!

Panel 4:
DOG MY CATS! YOU IS DONE ASSASSINATED MY TAIL BONE!
YOU WAS A-WINGLIN' IT TO THE MUSIC ----I WAS CARRIED AWAY.

POGO

by Walt Kelly

MAY 20, 1949

Panel 1:
- YOU CAUGHT ENOUGH FISH, POGO. HALF FOR YOU AND HALF FOR FRIENDLY OL' ME.
- HOWLAN' OWL, DO THIS LOOK LIKE FIFTY PERCENT TO YOU?
- POGO, MY BOY, THAT LOOK LIKE **ONE HUNDRED** PER CENT.

Panel 3:
- FIFTY PER CENT IS MO' OR LESS LIKE THIS HERE.

Panel 4:
- A FAIR DEAL FO' ALL IS OUR MOTTO.
- LET'S SEE, YOU SUB-DIVIDES THE MULTI-PLICATION BY THE SQUARE HEAD OF THE HIPPOPOTANEWS AND LUNK OFF THE FRICTIONS AND THE FRACTIONS THEN --- BZZZ --MM--HM--

MAY 21, 1949

Panel 1:
- ALBERT, OL' OWL AND TURTLE DEE-VIDES UP TWO FISHES I CAUGHT AN' I GETS HALF-- DO THIS LOOK LIKE HALF?
- POGO, YOU GOTTA GIVE IT A LI'L' OL' SCIENTIFIC TEST.
- POGO

Panel 2:
- IN YOU OWN HOUSE I WILL ANALYZE THE BOY WITH A COUPLE FEW TURNIP GREENS.

Panel 3:
- YESSIR! IT TASTE LIKE YOU IS GOT A FULL FIFTY PERCENT.

Panel 4:
- NOW YOU CAN WASH THE DISHES KNOWIN' YOU IS BEEN **UTTER** PRO-TECTED BY SCIENCE FROM **ANY** DOUBLE-DEALIN'.
- HOW CAN I EVER THANK YOU?

53

 **POGO** *by Walt Kelly*

MAY 23, 1949

WHEN YOU PORKY-PINES WANTS TO HUG YOU CHILLUNS -- HOW YOU MANAGE IT?

DON'T HUG.

DON'T LIKE *ANYBODY* GOOD ENOUGH TO HUG 'EM.

DOES YOU EVER ROLL OVER IN BED AND STICK YOU'SELF?

YES! AND I'M *GLAD!* SERVES ME RIGHT.

DON'T LIKE *ANYBODY.*

MAY 24, 1949

HOWDY, MISTUH CRANE - GONE HAVE A LI'L' OL' NAP?

FAUGH! WHAT A SHODDY IMITATION OF NATURE! - WHY ISN'T THIS CRANE ACTIN' LIKE A CRANE?

CRANES NAP ON ONE FOOT --- IN THE WATER - HEAD UNDER WING.

LIKE THIS?

HA!

JES' LET'S YOU STICK TO PORKYPININ' AN' I WILL BE A CRANE WITHOUT NO OUTSIDE HELP.

54

MAY 25, 1949

MAY 26, 1949

POGO

by Walt Kelly

MAY 27, 1949

IT'S A LETTER FOR YOU FROM A LADY, POGO.

MIND IF *I* READ *MY* LETTER OVER *YOUR* SHOULDER, MAILMAN?

ONCE I, TOO, RECEIVED BILLETS-DOUX... GENTLE MISSIVES OF ESTEEM FROM A FAIR ACQUAINTANCE.

YOU, PORKYPINE?

AYE-- BUT SHE MAINTAINED A DISCREET DISTANCE-- CLAIMED IT WAS A SCANDAL FOR ME TO APPROACH TOO CLOSE.

SHE WAS COLD-HEARTED?

SIR, ~ SHE WAS A **BALLOON** DANCER.

WALT KELLY

MAY 28, 1949

THIS LADY WROTE A LETTER SAYIN' "WHY DOESN'T OL' POGO ACT MORE LIKE A POSSUM? HAVE HIM CLIMB A TREE AND HANG BY HIS TAIL."

GOOD IDEA, GO AHEAD.

S'POSE I WROTE TO THE LADY, "HOW WOULD *YOU* LIKE TO GO CLIMB A TREE AN'----"

I IS MORE THE HUMAN BEAN TYPE-- THIS A JOB FOR A MONKEY.

DON'T BE FEARED-- I WILL BREAK YOUR FALL, IF ANY.

WELL UH--THANK YOU JUS' THE SAME, PORKYPINE--I'D RATHER FALL ON MY BARE-HEADED BRAIN.

WALT KELLY

MAY 30, 1949

MAY 31, 1949

POGO

by Walt Kelly

JUNE 1, 1949

JUNE 2, 1949

POGO

by Walt Kelly

JUNE 6, 1949

HERE, ALBERT, DRINK ALL THIS WATER AN' IT WILL RAISE THE TIDE LEVEL INSIDE OF YOU.

NOW THE WATER SHOULD BE UP NEAR YOUR EYE-BRIARS AN' WE CAN SKUM OFF THAT LI'L OL' POLLYWOG YOU IS SWALLOWED.

YEP! HERE HE COME! EASY NOW!....AHA.... **GOT HIM!**

THERE, SEE HOW SIMPLE? NOT SO HARD ONCE WE PUTS OUR MINDS TO IT!

BLUB

JUNE 7, 1949

HELLO, OL' PORKYPINE, WE IS TAKIN' CARE OF OL' POLLYWOG BOY.

LOOK NOT AGHAST. I, TOO, AM A BABY SITTER.

BUT REVILED AND SLANDERED BY MY CLIENTELE "--AH, SLANDER WHOSE STING IS SHARPER THAN THE SWORD."

YOU IS MORE OR LESS POINTY YOU'SELF.

COME, MY BOY. IT'S BACK TO THE MINES.

SIT EASY, MR. PINE.

LUCKY THING IT'S OLD HARD-BACK TURTLE'S LI'L BOY HE'S TAKIN' CARE OF.

POGO

by *Walt Kelly*

JUNE 8, 1949

JUNE 9, 1949

JUNE 10, 1949

JUNE 11, 1949

JUNE 13, 1949

GIT ON HOME AN' GIT WASHED, CHILD.

I'M **NOT** YOUR CHILD! I'M SAM, THE NATURAL BORN TURTLE.

POOR SAM! HE'S SO MUDDY, MIS' HOP FROG THINKS HE'S HER LI'L BOY.

LET'S LOOK FOR THE CHILD.

GREAT! GREAT! POGO IS SIGNAL THAT HE GOT HOLD OF THE LOST TAD POLE.

DOG MY CATS! YOU IS CAUGHT MY TOE BONE!

MAN! I IS WONDER WHERE TAD GITS FOUR LI'L FRIENDS SO QUICK!

JUNE 14, 1949

DOG BONE! EVERY TIME I LOOKS UNDERNEATH OF THE SWAMP WATER FO' THE LI'L LOST TAD POLE I PUTS OUT MY SEE-GAR. WHAT **YOU** GIGGLIN' 'BOUT?

HEE HEE

OH I IS JUS' FEEL **EE**-NORMOUS TICKLED.

YOU ACTIN' MIGHTY CALLOUS---SNICKERIN' AND WINGLIN' WHILST A POOR LI'L OL' POLLYWOG-----HA! I THOUGHT SO!

THE LOST IS FOUND! YOU WAS HARBORIN' THE FROG CHILD!

POGO

JUNE 15, 1949

JUNE 16, 1949

POGO

by *Walt Kelly*

JUNE 17, 1949

H'LO OL' PORKYPINE – SET YOU DOWN AN' USE MY BAIT. FIGGER US GONE HAVE GOOD FISHIN' WEATHER?

WITHOUT ACCESS TO METEOROLOGICAL STATIONS OR WIND VELOCITY FIGURED BY THEODOLITE OR ANALYSIS OF THE ISOBAR FIELD IT IS DIFFICULT TO SAY.

MY PROGNOSIS (WITH NO KNOWLEDGE OF FRONT MOVEMENTS) WOULD BE A MINIMUM OF PRECIPITATION OR EVEN A SEASONAL ARIDITY.

IT ISN'T HURT NONE TO BE CIVIL, YOU KNOW.

JUNE 18, 1949

PORKYPINE, YOU OUGHT TO LAUGH MORE – HERE'S A OL' JOKE FOR YOU: A GOAT LOSE HIS NOSE – – MAN SAY, "HOW **DO** HE SMELL?" OTHER MAN SAY, "**BAD AS EVER!**" HOO-HOO HOO-HEE!

THANK YOU VERY MUCH.

THIS IS A HUMOROUS ANECDOTE. A GOAT LOST HIS NOSE – THE FIRST MAN SAYS, "WHAT WILL HE SMELL WITH NOW?" THE OTHER REPLIES, "AS BAD AS EVER." HAW HAW HAW?

IT'S REASONABLE TO ASSUME THE EMPLOYES OF A COMIC STRIP SHOULD HAVE **SOME** SENSE OF HUMOR – PUNY AN' PLEBIAN THOUGH IT MIGHT BE.

JUNE 20, 1949

WORM BOY! I GONE PLAY HOOKEY TODAY AN' GO FISHIN'-- COME ON 'LONG.

NOSSIR, POGO POSSUM!

THE KING OF PATAGONIA IS WAITIN' LUNCH FO' ME -- BESIDES WHEN **YOU** GO FISHIN'-----

I ISN'T THE BOY WHAT ACHES TO PLAY **HOOKEY** WITH YOU.

NOBODY KNOW THE ANGLES LIKE A LI'L OL' FRIENDLY WIGGLE WORM.

JUNE 21, 1949

HELP HELP HELP HELP HELP HELP HELP HELP HELP HELP

DOES YOU GOT TIME, A BOY YONDER SEEM TO HAVE A PRESSIN' NEED FOR HELP.

WHAT'S THE FUSS 'BOUT, HOUN' DOG?

I'M TRAPPED! CAUGHT! ENSNARED IN A FIENDISH **DEE**-VICE OF THE HUNTSMAN! HELP·HELP.

LIFT UP YOUR NATURAL BORN FOOT!

SAVED!!

POGO

by Walt Kelly

JUNE 22, 1949

A KISS FOR YOU! PART OF A DEVOTED SERVICE THAT IS YOURS HENCE-FORTH FROM MAN'S BEST FRIEND, TO WIT, THE DOG!

SPLOO

GO 'WAY, TO WIT!

AH, INDEED, YOU SAVED MY LIFE, SIRRAH! BULLY FOR YOU! NEVER SHALL I LEAVE YOU! *NEVER!* BULLY, INDEED!

WHAT'S SO NATURAL BORN BULLY BOUT THAT?

THINK OF IT-- A LOVING DOG ALWAYS BESIDE YOU!

CHOMP CHOMP- *ALWAYS!*

I IS DUE TO BUST OUT IN SMALL POX, YOU KNOW.

WALT KELLY

JUNE 23, 1949

NOW HERE IS A CHARMING OPERATION-- THE FAITHFUL DOG WELCOMES HOME THE MASTER -- WATCH THIS---

POGO

NOW, EASY, BOY.

BEHOLD HOW THE LOVING ANIMAL SPRUCES UP THE HOME-COMING -- *WELCOME WELCOME!*

AN ENDEARING GESTURE, EH? OOPS.

YOU IS TRIPPED!

IF YOU IS GOT ANY MORE ENDEARING CHARACTER-ISTICS -- WE IS BOTH GONE BE *DEE*-STROYED!

WALT KELLY

POGO

by Walt Kelly

JUNE 24, 1949

JUNE 25, 1949